CLEVELAND
CAVALIERS

DAN ZADRA

CREATIVE EDUCATION

Photo Credit: Creative Education would like to thank NBA photographer Ron Koch (New York City) for the color photography in this series.

Published by Creative Education Inc., 123 South Broad Street, Mankato, Minnesota 56001.

ISBN: 0-88682-200-9

Looming like a brilliant diamond on the shores of Lake Erie is the proud city of Cleveland, Ohio. It is a thriving metropolis, a place recently described by an economist as a "magnet for Midwest movers and shakers."

Cleveland is the biggest city in Ohio, thanks in part to John D. Rockefeller. The wealthy industrialist started his Standard Oil dynasty near the mouth of Cleveland's Cuyahoga River in 1870. It was a bold and imaginative venture, an example of "big thinking" that soon sparked similar ideas in the minds of Rockefeller's neighbors.

Over the next hundred years or so, the diligent citizens of Cleveland built their city into a powerful ore port and bustling Great Lakes shipping point. Nationally respected colleges, museums and art centers sprang up among the skyscrapers. Tree-lined boulevards and more than 2,000 acres of parks were installed to bring serenity and beauty to a city on the move.

For such a city, big league sports became a must. The Cleveland Indians baseball team was launched in 1901. In 1946, the Cleveland Browns football club took off under the direction of legendary coach Paul Brown. Both teams have won world championships.

On February 7, 1970, pro basketball finally came to town. A syndicate of wealthy men, headed by colorful Cleveland businessman Nicholas Mileti, paid $3.7-million for the right to install the Cleveland Cavaliers as the 18th team in the NBA.

Now the pressure was on. Mileti and his partners already knew how tough it would be for a new team like the Cavaliers to establish itself in a league dominated by living legends such as Jerry West, Walt Frazier, Wilt Chamberlain, Bill Russell, Willis Reed, Elgin Baylor and Hal Greer. But there was the additional pressure of playing in a city with such a strong football and baseball tradition. Or, as Mileti put it, "of measuring up to the Browns and Indians."

The senior member of the Cavs, Phil Hubbard finished the 1987-88 season among the club's all-time leaders in rebounds, points and minutes played.

Bill Fitch, the man chosen to be the Cavs' first head coach, was an optimistic sort of guy. But Fitch had been around the NBA long enough to know that the Cleveland fans shouldn't expect miracles from a first year club. After all, Fitch's team would be drawn from a pool of inexperienced NBA subs or older players whose heyday had passed. "Just remember," he reminded the fans, "my name is Fitch, not Houdini."

Coach Fitch wisely started with a man in the middle, selecting four-year veteran center Walt Wesley from Chicago. Wesley, a good all-around player, stood out in any crowd. His trademark was a flaming burnt-orange Afro hairstyle.

Next, the Cavaliers snatched up Bobby Smith, a deadly outside shooter who was appropriately nicknamed "Bingo." Guard Butch Beard was also acquired, but he still had a one year commitment to fulfill with a larger, more powerful squad, the United States Army. Beard would join the Cavs' lineup the following year.

Meanwhile, Fitch gave Wesley and rookie forward John Johnson the green light to set the pace for the club. Wesley's chief weapons were a nifty turnaround fadeaway shot and an all-out kamikaze style of rebounding. He became the team's leading rebounder and scorer, including a sizzling single game high of 50 points against the Royals.

Explosive Bobby Smith, a deadly outside shooter, was a member of the Cavaliers' very first team in 1970.

Johnson, nicknamed "J.J.," dished off slick feeds to teammates when he was double-covered and somehow skimmed in his peculiar jump shots if he was open. When J.J. shot, his feet barely left the floor. The arc of his shot was flat but the ball usually rippled the net. A wily defender, Johnson became Fitch's rover, playing different positions from game to game to shut down the other team's top scorer.

Unfortunately, Johnson and Wesley provided just about the only highlights in the Cavs' charter season. Cleveland lost 15 games in a row before winning their first, 105-103 against Portland, another expansion team. A mere 14 additional wins would follow for the entire season. The futility experienced by the players was epitomized the night John Warren got confused and scored two points for Portland by making a layup in the wrong basket.

The only way to go was up, and that's the direction the Cavaliers took the next season. Their record jumped to 23-59, thanks in large part to the appearance of Austin Carr. The proverbial scoring machine, Carr had averaged 34.5 points a game during his collegiate career at Notre Dame. The Cavaliers drafted him as the second choice overall in the NBA draft, and he rewarded them by ringing the bell for 21.2 points a

Austin Carr

"Austin has certainly made my job easier. The man can flat-out fill the hoop," Fitch pointed out.

game, good enough to earn a spot on the All-Rookie Team.

Combined with Butch Beard, now back from the Army, the hard-driving Carr helped give the Cavaliers one of the league's most respected back-courts. "Austin has certainly made my job easier," Fitch pointed out. "The man can flat-out fill the hoop."

Cleveland's second year record might have been drastically better if Carr hadn't been sidelined after 43 games with a broken foot. It was a tough break for the Cavs, but they would bounce back in fine form the following year.

Butch Beard

During the off-season, Fitch engineered an excellent trade, sending young Butch Beard to Seattle in exchange for Lenny Wilkens, a wiry little playmaker. Wilkens, a perennial All-Star, could do it all. Dare him to shoot from outside and he would oblige you with his old-fashioned one-handed set shot. Play him tight and he'd explode around you, drive the lane, toss up a little shovel shot or hit an open teammate with a pass. He was the ideal floor general for Fitch's team.

"I think with some of the younger guys we can surprise a lot of people this year," Wilkens said on the day of the deal. "This isn't an expansion team anymore, at least it doesn't have to be."

With Wilkens calling the plays, Cleveland climbed to 32-50 in 1972-73. They were losing their baby teeth and by now even the NBA powerhouses were feeling the Cavs' new bite. Boston, Milwaukee and Los Angeles, the

---

"It's not how you start that counts," said Wilkens. "It's how you finish."

---

league's elite three, all dropped games to the hustling young Cavaliers.

The team showed character, too. When the Cavs got off to a rough start in 1973-74, losing 15 of their first 19 games, no one panicked. "It's not how you start that counts," said Wilkens. "It's how you finish."

Campy Russell (21) and the Lakers'
Don Ford (35) tangle in 1977 action.

By mid-season, the Cavs were back in the groove again. Not that they were regarded as favorites over teams like the Celtics or Bucks, but there was a new realization that a game against Cleveland was no longer a night off.

Wilkens, playing in the last complete season of his illustrious career, averaged 16.4 points and Carr snapped the twine for his usual 22. The Cavs' soft spot was at center where Fitch played musical chairs with 6-foot-8 Jim Brewer, a natural power forward; 6-foot-9 Steve Patterson, a plodding backup; and 7-foot Luke Witte, a raw rookie.

All in all, though, the Cavaliers were still a tough team to handle. The defending champion New York Knicks learned that lesson first-hand. The Cavs dismantled the Knicks, 114-92, in their final game at ancient Cleveland Arena. Seven months later, the doors would swing open on the Cavs' new home, the handsome Coliseum in nearby suburban Richfield. There, a bright new chapter in the Cavaliers' history would commence.

A spanking new arena seemed fitting for a team with a new look. Wilkens had turned in his sneakers after the 1973-74 campaign, but there were several young up-and-comers who were anxious to take his place. The Cavs traded for sharpshooting Dick Snyder and drafted Campy Russell and Clarence "Foots" Walker. Asked by a reporter to describe the collegiate careers of Russell and Walker, coach Fitch replied with a wink: "They graduated with honors from the college of Slick and Fast." Enough said.

■

*All-pro guard Lenny Wilkens watches a 1972
Cavalier game from the stands. The next day
Wilkens joined the Cavs as a player.*

Sixteen games into the 1974-75 season, Austin Carr went down with a knee injury, but the Cavs hung tough. Coming down to the wire, the club actually found itself in contention for its first-ever playoff berth. Only two games remained in the regular season, and the Cavaliers would have to win both to stay alive.

Now the Cleveland fans came out in record numbers. More than 20,000 people poured through the turnstiles at Richfield Coliseum to watch the Cavs take on the Knicks in the first of the final two do-or-die match-ups. As each of the Cavaliers was introduced that evening, he was greeted by a thunderous standing ovation. Onlookers saw tears in the eyes of owner Nick Mileti and coach Fitch, who were no doubt recalling the sparse but faithful crowds of the old Arena days. The Cavs rewarded their fans by thumping the Knicks, and Jim Brewer provided the icing with a monstrous dunk in the closing moments.

As it turned out, the Cavs were nipped in game two, 95-94, by the Kansas City Kings. A nationwide television audience watched the Cavaliers hang their heads as they

walked off the court. The players were disappointed but not ashamed. After all, their 40-42 record that season was a franchise best and a promising jump-off point for an even better season just ahead.

First, however, Fitch had some unfinished business to attend to. Shoring up that shaky center position was a must if the Cavaliers expected to compete with the NBA's best. It was rumored that Fitch had his eye on veteran Chicago Bulls center Nate "The Great" Thurmond. No one really expected the Bulls to let Nate loose, but they did.

A six-time All-Star, the 6-foot-11 Thurmond had led his previous teams to nine playoff appearances in 12 NBA seasons. Though he was supposed to be past his prime, the balding giant was still considered one of the game's top defensive centers. "I'll guarantee you, Nate still makes life miserable for me," said Kareem Abdul-Jabbar in tribute.

With Thurmond providing the inspiration, the Cavaliers powered their way up the Central Division ladder in 1975-76 and into the playoffs for the first time. Thurmond played like a kid again. Time after time, he stifled the enemy's inside game and cleaned the boards with a vengeance. No longer looked to as a scorer, Thurmond relished his role as a frightening defensive specialist. Cavalier fans called him "Dr. Defense."

No longer looked to as a scorer, Thurmond relished his role as a frightening defensive specialist.

Thurmond and company not only reached the playoffs, they did so as the team with the number one regular season record in the Central Divsion at 49-33, and all this in just their sixth season in the league.

After gettting a bye in the first round, the Cavaliers took on the Washington Bullets in what eventually developed into a titanic series. The Cavs lost the first game but evened the series in Game 2 on a magnificent, buzzer beating 30-footer by Bingo Smith. Back and forth it went, ultimately coming down to the final seconds of the seventh and deciding game. That's when Dick Snyder took over. He hit a running five-footer off the backboard that gave the Cavs a stunning 87-85 triumph and sent the fans streaming onto the floor to mob their heroes.

Next up were the big, bad Boston Celtics who must have been wondering, "Who are these guys?" They soon found out.

As expected, the Celtics won the first two games on the famous parquet floor at Boston Garden. Then the series swung to Cleveland's Richfield Coliseum where the Cavalier fans took over. At times it seemed as if everyone in northern Ohio had brought an air gun to the game. Inspired, the Cavs bounced back to win two straight and even the series. But time was running out on Cleveland's Cinderella season. The Celtics hit their notorious championship stride over the next two games, winning not only the Cavalier series but eventually their 13th NBA title as well.

■

Ron Harper, the Cavs' 1986 first round draft choice, went on to become the all-time leading rookie scorer in Cavs' history.

Still, it had been a satisfying season for the Cavaliers. Once the laughingstock of the league, they had proven once and for all that they belonged on the same court with the best in the world. Fitch was named the NBA's Coach of the Year, and he threw a gala dinner to share the credit with each of his players. It was a happy time for all. But trouble lay just ahead.

The unspoken fear that lingers in the mind of every NBA coach and player is the fear of serious injury. At any given moment under the basket, there may be as many as five or six men who collectively weigh in at more than a half-ton, all vying for possession of a little leather ball.

. . . they belonged on the same court with the best in the world.

Jim Chones

"Sometimes I just close my eyes and pray," said coach Fitch. "I look out there and see ten or twelve size 15 shoes leaping up and down on a little five-foot patch of floor under the hoop and I cringe at what could happen. I tell you, there have been times when I was too far away to see a player get hurt, but I could actually hear something break."

Through the first half of the 1970s the Cavaliers had remained relatively healthy. Beginning with the 1976-77 season, however, Lady Luck began a three-year holiday at the Cavs' expense. Riding the momentum of their playoff success the year before, Cleveland roared into 1976 with a streak of 16 victories in their first 20 games. Then Jim Chones went down with a broken foot. Campy Russell and Jim Cleamons were the next to go. Finally, on February 8, Nate the Great suffered a serious knee injury which, except for a brief appearance in the playoffs, would end his phenomenal career.

So the Cavaliers limped home with identical 43-39 regular season records in both 1976-77 and 1977-78. In both years they entered the first round of the playoffs with their top five starters wrapped up like mummies in ace bandages and tape. Both years they were easily bounced out of the first-round mini-series.

Elmore Smith

When fresh troops were brought in, the injured list just grew longer. By 1978-79, Walt Frazier and Elmore Smith had both claimed starting positions with the Cavs. Frazier, a guard extraordinaire known for his flashy clothes and even flashier ball-handling, raised everyone's expectations before falling to a virus in mid-season. Next, the 7-foot Smith, who had rejected an astounding 176 shots the year before, was toppled by a knee injury.

Not surprisingly, Cleveland plummeted all the way to 30-52 and failed to make the playoffs. coach Fitch, the Cavs' first and only coach up to that point, was discouraged. He resigned at season's end, handing the coaching reins to Stan Albeck.

Coach Albeck, a former Los Angeles Lakers assistant under Jerry West, did his best to re-start the Cavs' engines in 1979-80. To spark the sluggish Cleveland offense, Albeck inserted 6-foot-9 rookie Mike Mitchell in the starting lineup. Mitchell responded like a seasoned pro, averaging 22 points, many of them scored by way of gravity defying slam dunks.

Coach Albeck, a former Los Angeles Lakers assistant . . . did his best to re-start the Cavs' engines in 1979-80.

Cavalier center Brad Daugherty can do it all, but tenacious rebounding, shot blocking and pin point passing are his hallmarks.

Aside from Mitchell's heroics, the Cavs remained flat and listless that year and were never really in playoff contention. The players themselves were distracted by disturbing rumors that the team was about to be sold. Would the Cavs' owner keep the team in Cleveland? Would certain players be traded away? Would Albeck still be the coach?

At the close of the 1979-80 season, the rumors gave way to the formal announcement by Mr. Mileti that he had indeed completed the sale of the team to mystery man Ted Stepien. The Cleveland fans were encouraged by the news that Stepien had both the money and the desire to acquire high-priced superstars for the Cavs, if necessary. Stepien's critics, and there would be more and more of them in the years to follow, pointed out that he was likely to make impulsive decisions even though he knew very little about the game of basketball. The net result would later be described by a Cleveland reporter as "turmoil in the front office, chaos on the court, and boredom in the stands."

Bluntly said, the early 1980s weren't very pretty years for the poor Cavaliers and their fans.

Bluntly said, the early 1980s weren't very pretty years for the poor Cavaliers and their fans. Under head coach Bill Musselman, the once proud Cavs fell to 28-54 in 1980-81. The following year, four different coaches shuffled in and shuffled out during a season that saw the club lurch its way to 67 defeats, including the league's longest losing streak, at 19.

Fly, Clyde, fly! Walt Frazier floats
through the air for two against
Chicago's Norm Van Lier. (1977)

There was a glimmer of progress in 1982-83. Veteran coach and former NBA great Tom Nissalke came in to lift the players' spirits and help them regain their confidence. The early season addition of World B. Free also helped considerably. The fun loving Free was outspoken and cocky, but he had the talent and moves to back up his boasts.

"There's no one can stop me, and I'm telling the truth," World would crow to the Cleveland reporters. "When I get hot, nobody can cool me down."

And he was right. Free got open often enough to average 23.9 points in 1982-83. His critics, however, said he could've averaged 30 with a little more work and a lot less talk. Free's teammate Cliff Robinson snagged an average of 11.1 rebounds that season. Aside from those two men, however, the Cavs had few players with decent stats and finished the year at 23-59, a modest eight-game improvement over the year before.

It wasn't until 1984-85 that the Cavaliers finally snapped out of their doldrums.

"The Cavs started 2-19 and everyone was saying, 'Same old Cleveland,' " wrote a columnist for *The Sporting News*. "Everyone was wrong. Rookie coach George Karl maintained faith in his system, got bundles of points from World B. Free, and quality inside play from Roy Hinson and Phil Hubbard. Karl directed the Cavs to the playoffs for the first time in seven years. Cleveland took Boston to four games before losing in the first round."

■ *Lenny Wilkens, one of the most popular Cavalier players during the early 1970s, returned to the club in 1985-86, this time as head coach.*

Believe it or not, Karl was fired the very next season, along with Cavalier general manager Harry Weltman. The axe fell in the wake of the Cavaliers' puzzling nosedive into the cellar at 29-53, but it triggered what would soon become a very positive rebuilding program.

From the 1986 college draft, the Cavaliers selected No. 1 pick Brad Daugherty, an imposing 7-foot center out of North Carolina. Their eighth pick yielded Miami of Ohio's Ron Harper, a 6-foot-6 shooting guard with three-point range and confidence.

Lenny Wilkens, a familiar face from the early days of the Cavalier franchise, was welcomed back to the fold in 1986-87. Old-time Cav fans recalled how Lenny's steady leadership as a playmaking guard had elevated the club to respectability during the early 1970s. Lenny had a few more gray hairs now, some of them earned no doubt during the late seventies when he had led the Seattle SuperSonics from nowhere to the top of the world.

■

Ron Harper, No. 4, stuffs one past a frustrated New Jersey Nets defender.

With Wilkens at the helm, the Cavs improved to 31-51 in 1986-87. The youngsters, Harper and Daugherty, topped the team in scoring, supported by outstanding efforts from forwards Phil Hubbard and John "Hot Rod" Williams.

Now add the names of 1987 rookie draft choice Mark Price and veteran Craig Ehlo to the roster. Wilkens said that both guards reminded him of Celtic legend Bob Cousy who was the kind of player who would scramble all the way into the cheap seats in pursuit of a loose ball.

The hustling paid off in 1987-88 when Wilkens' Cavaliers ran up a 41-40 record and returned to the playoffs. A fluke? Don't bet on it. According to Denver Nuggets head coach Doug Moe, "Anyone who thinks the new Cavaliers bear any resemblance to the old club is making a grand mistake. We fear them every time we play them. They have so much talent. Talent, talent,

---

"Anyone who thinks the new Cavs bear any resemblance to the old club is making a grand mistake."

---

talent. Once they mature, they're going to grab a lot of headlines."

In the 1988 playoffs, the Cavs squared off with the Chicago Bulls and their high-flying superstar Michael Jordan. Ehlo shadowed Jordan on defense and held him below his average for two straight games. Sure, the Bulls eventually emerged as narrow winners of the five-game series, but eliminate a few youthful mistakes by the

■
Signed by the Cavs as a free agent in 1987, versatile swingman Craig Ehlo was nicknamed "Mr Everything" for his ability to play three positions.

Cavaliers and the series would've surely swung the other way.

Wilkens, a man who steers away from big talk or bravado, couldn't conceal the sparkle in his eyes when discussing the Cavaliers' progress and what was supposed to be a disappointing end to the season.

"Personally, I wish we were heading back to training camp tomorrow morning," said Wilkens with a hint of a smile. "It's been said before, but this team is a team of the future. Give us a little more time, and I think you'll be pleasantly surprised."

■